Gifts
OF THE
SPIRIT

Gifts
OF THE
SPIRIT

**CHRISTIAN
FREE VERSE**

CAROL GUNZELMANN

gatekeeper press
Columbus, Ohio

GIFTS OF THE SPIRIT
Christian Free Verse

Published by Gatekeeper Press
2167 Stringtown Rd, Suite 109
Columbus, OH 43123-2989
www.GatekeeperPress.com

Library of Congress Control Number: 2022943917

ISBN (paperback): 9781662931345
eISBN: 9781662931352

Contents

Gifts of the Spirit

Words too "right" to be my own,
Insights beyond intellect,
Guidance past uncertainty,
Momentum through pain and fear,
Serenity in turmoil,

Comfort amidst life's sorrows,
Forgiveness blind to my guilt,
Hope radiant in dark times,
Power against helplessness,
Love sufficient for all voids.

The Ultimate Gift

God's grace is the ultimate gift,
purchased with His son's blood,
yet freely given to me,
in amazing abundance.

Let it fill my soul and overflow
into my thoughts, words, and deeds.

In God We Gain

In God we gain
grace and integrity to overcome our sinfulness,
faith and trust to quiet our doubts,
strength and power to conquer our fears,
mercy and healing to ease our suffering,
comfort and peace to lighten our sadness,
meaning and hope to live our lives.

Busy

I look without seeing,
hear without listening,
touch without feeling,
taste and smell without savoring.

Yet God's love is everywhere,
for all my senses--
in the beauty of nature,
in the abundance of resources,
in the diversity of His children,
in the products of creativity.

I allow everyday busy-ness
to steal my sensitivities
away from knowing
His rich blessings.
Lord, open my being to live
always fully aware,
treasuring Your abiding love.

Invitation

Come, child,
You invite the little child to come.
But she vanished decades ago,
stifled by shame, beaten down.

I yearn to see again through her eyes,
discovering everything for the first time,
awe-struck, wondering, delighting;
being, not doing -- my quest;
my heart trusting and hopeful, open.
Take my hand; show me the way, Father.

Point of View

When I'm convinced
evil prevails,
I'm overwhelmed.
My soul despairs,
and my heart aches.
I ask, "Where is God?
Doesn't He care?"

When I realize
goodness abounds,
I'm empowered
to do God's work
and know His love.
God is present!
His grace is mine!

In God's Eyes

Broken and lonely, I climbed onto God's lap,
shame casting my gaze downward.
But Spirit prodded me to persist.
Again and again, the Father beckoned,
"Come to me, my beloved child."

And then one day, it happened.
When I dared to look up,
I saw His tears of joy.
Often now I seek out those eyes
to see a love that surpasses human
and know that I am enough.

Abuser

Abuser steals innocence,
beats down ego,
creates fear,
but cannot touch the soul!

God nurtures integrity,
feeds the spirit,
keeps it strong.
The soul belongs to God!

The Swing

Little girl innocent
has been touched by evil
she cannot comprehend.

On the edge of the woods
dangles a thick rope swing,
a notched board for a seat.

There she swings--
toes leave earth,
touch the clouds.

And she sings--
from her soul
to God's ear,

till she feels in her heart
the calm she's been needing.

Grown now, at times I return
to thoughts of younger days.

I remember the swing
and the girl that I was
and how she's with me still.

Though my fears are different
and my innocence gone,
the need is always there.

But I learned long ago,
when my soul sings to God,
the blessed calm is mine.

Anger

Anger bursts in—
dark, cold, putrid.
I want to deny the intruder,
but it demands to be heard.

The unwelcome visitor sneers-
a reminder of my powerlessness.
Pushed down, it eats away at me.
Released, it hurts others.

Yet resist I cannot.
For to be rid of it,
I must deal with it.
That's humanity's necessity.

It turns me against people,
so that I can forgive.
It lashes out at God,
so my faith is strengthened.

It leaves me transformed.
Yet the next time it erupts,
no gratitude is remembered.
There are lessons yet to learn.

Death

We name death
a departure, passing, demise,
end-of-life culmination,
finality.

Christ makes death
a homecoming, welcome, newness,
butterfly transformation,
eternity.

Loss

How can I face the day
when I have lost so much?
Have You forsaken me
when I needed You most?
Am I being punished?

But losing faith would be
an even greater loss.
I surrender to You,
and with time and prayer,
anger subsides, heart heals,
tears dry, and life goes on.

The Knotted Cord

O, God!
I did it again—
that thing I hate
about myself,
that thing I promised
I'd never do again.

How could you
possibly love me now?

But while I wallowed
in self-loathing,
You took the frayed ends
of the strained cord
that had held me to You,
where now my sin
had caused a tear,
and with grace and love,
You knotted them together
to draw me closer
to You.

Thank You, God!
You did it again!

Promises

Whatever God asks,
He has promised me
guidance, sustenance,
resources, wisdom,
power, faithfulness,
insights, joy, and grace
sufficient for it.

Because I have faith...

If my soul yearns to know the sweetness
of His peace, I must surrender.
When my heart longs to feel the power
of His love, I have to be open.
Because my mind wants to comprehend the depth
of His grace, I humbly repent.
Yet I realize my efforts bring only a foretaste
of the promised eternity.

Choice

In God's name…
differences, commonalities.
division, unity.
discord, harmony.
war, peace—
our choice.

Bad Things Happen

(I cry to God,)
"Bad things happen
to good people.

Abuse, disease,
violence, hate,
wars, disasters
leave their scars,
claim our loved ones
before their time.

I must wonder,
God, where are You?
Why don't You stop
this suffering?"

(And God replies,)
"In my wisdom,
as your Father,
with steadfast love,
I have granted
each child free will.

Know I'm present,
often saddened
by the choices
my children make.

I've sent angels
(Don't you notice?)
to make of bad
a greater good.

Love will triumph;
this I promise.
Peace will be yours,
my beloved child.
Fear not; have faith."

In the Broken Places

God, You don't protect me from all the world's evil.
Failures, troubles, and hurts inevitably come my way.
But because You intend good for me,
You are there to help me through it,
and make me wiser, healthier,
stronger in the broken places.

Prayer for the Broken

May your wounds be portals
for all God's goodness—
mercy, love, and healing—
to fill every cell
with hope and peace.

Forgiveness

Hurt people hurt people.
With God's grace I have learned
forgiveness is a choice
to take away the hurt
and to stop hurting others.
It unburdens my heart
to live a grace-filled life.

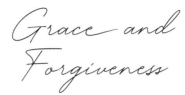

Grace and Forgiveness

forgiven—grace received
forgiving—grace bestowed
empowered, unburdened,
freed and blessed

Father God

Because God is my Father, I am never alone:
He guides me through life's perils;
He comforts me in my sorrows;
He quiets my fears;
He brings light to my dark times.

Because God is my Father, I am loved:
He writes love notes everywhere in creation;
He loves me even when I cannot love myself;
He cannot love me more and will not love me less;
He calls me beloved, unworthy and sinful as I am.

Because God is my Father, I am blessed:
He gives me in abundance everything I need;
He wants nothing but good for me;
He sends angels to care for me;
He forgives my sins into eternity.

Holy Arithmetic

The Trinity—three undivided;
Father counts my hairs but not my sins,
Son has taken away death's power,
the Spirit adds meaning to my life.
My blessings are multiplied each day.

Transformation

God's love transforms

a seeker of truth
into a believer,

a hopeless sinner
into a thankful saint,

a cold, selfish heart
into a generous soul,

a crude wooden cross
into the tree of life.

Journey to Easter

We walked the rugged road to Gogotha,
Jesus and I.
Along the way, I waved a palm branch,
hailed Him my king.

But I am a sinful creature,
and it was my indiscretions
He decried in the temple.
It was my feet He washed
while my betrayals He foretold.
So it was my perverse voice
that shouted, "Crucify Him!"

I bore the weight of the cross
up Calvary's hill.
I placed the crown made of thorns
upon His head.

Yet through all His suffering,
He prayed for me.

Nails that pierced His hands and feet
left their marks upon my soul.
I knew at the empty tomb
that Christ died and rose for me.

Shadow of the Cross

In the shadow
of the cross is
unfailing love,
sustaining hope,
life beyond death,
my salvation,
eternity.

So I live with
adoration,
indebtedness,
prayer on my lips,
faith in my soul,
love in my heart.

At the Cross

In His eyes no trace of fear,
I see only compassion.
He says, "Father, forgive them,
for they know not what they do."
He prays for me from the cross,
then gives His life for my sins.
To reserve my place in Heaven.
I need only believe and repent.

My heart aches with profound love—
that, however, diminished
by God's perfect love for me.
So my life should be a prayer
of eternal gratitude.

Jesus Gave

Mocked,
taunted.
crucified,
on the cross,
Jesus gave
love,
comfort,
forgiveness,
eternity.

Love Guaranteed

As a child of God,
willful,
sinful,
shameful
though I am,
I am loved
abundantly,
unconditionally,
eternally.

I cannot comprehend, but I know
because that same love for me
held His Son to Calvary's cross.

Those People

Their looks frighten me.
Their words offend me.
Their touch annoys me.
Their deeds repulse me.

They're God's dear children.
They're Jesus' lost sheep.
They're ones I pass by.
They're those I should love.

There help the needy.
There lift poor spirits.
There share your blessings.
There be God's servant.

Sight

Father, Your children are diverse and unique—
in Your eyes, none better than any other.
Give us that sight that knows no hate, only joy,
so differences inform, enrich the world.

Come and See

In my mind, come and see
an acceptance of my own powerlessness.

In my heart, come and see
a love that reflects God's love.

In my soul, come and see
a peace created by God's grace.

Come and see Jesus stays in me.

God's Child

As God's child, I am
loved to be loving,
forgiven to be forgiving
blessed to be a blessing.

Songlare

Because Songlare is in my eyes
I see needs and injustices
that call out for my attention.
My Sonlit soul counts my blessings
and compels me to do God's work
to make the world a better place.

Son Sun

When life is hard,
and I can't see the sun
for the darkening clouds,
let me see the Son
for His unfailing love.

Sonlight

Sonlight
touches my heart,
lifts my spirit,
focuses my mind,
empowers my body
to do God's will.

Walking in the Sonlight

Shadows fall behind me.
God's path is clear to me,
and I am not alone.
There is purpose and joy,
security and hope,
walking in the Sonlight.

Nature

colors,
patterns,
beauty,

movement,
textures,
warmth,

fragrances,
melodies,
harmonies,

stillness,
gentleness,
simplicity,

intricacy,
intensity,
power--
love notes from God.

Today I found a love note from God
He tucked it away for me to find.
It was just for me; it made me smile!
My grateful response, "I love You too!"

Stream

The stream of God's love
washes over life's debris
and floods into my heart.

Leaves

A falling leaf
from God's hand to mine
inspires awe and gratitude.

Under my feet
its rustling fellows
tell of the cycle of life.

God in nature—
constant reminders
of His creative power.

Song of Joy

The Lord celebrates me with a song of joy.
Its rhythm is in the beating of my heart.
Its melody echoes above the world's noise.
Its harmonies resonate through my limbs.
Intimate music for a wretched sinner!

Spiritual Dance

When I ask, God blesses.
When I fear, God empowers.
When I fall, God lifts.
When I sin, God pardons.
When I can't, God does.

Believe and be generous,
oh, my soul.

When I serve, God welcomes.
When I trust, God fulfills.
When I succeed, God rejoices.
When I forgive, God sanctifies.
When I do, God perfects.

The Parting of the Mists

When the mists of egocentrism part,
God is there, always and forever.
So that farthest from His will,
I am closest to His amazing grace.

God Wastes Nothing

Though Satan may have power,
God has authority.
He can turn bad choices
to opportunities
beyond our boldest prayers.
Thank God, God wastes nothing!

Anger brings forgiveness.
Pain fosters compassion.
Fears reveal hidden strengths.
Doubts lead to renewal.
Failures teach us lessons.
Thank God, God wastes nothing!

God is Grace

Because God is, grace is.
                Grace is freely given
because God paid the price.
        God, help me to live in,
               through,
               within,
               out of,
                     knowing,
                     accepting,
                     responding to,
                     extending

        that grace.

Amazing Grace

God's amazing grace,
purchased with Christ's blood,
is given freely
and abundantly.
It cannot be earned
nor ever withheld.
When you accept it
humbly, gratefully
the Holy Spirit
works in and through you.

A Life as Prayer

With every breath Your grace allows,
I seek a life lived as a prayer—
with gratitude, humility,
obedience, and joyfulness—
faithfully and generously,
imploring Your grace and mercy
in all I do, on all I meet.

They Will Know You

I pray they know You because they know me—
God-given blessings shared generously,
mercy and goodness echoed in my words,
Your grace reflected in all my actions,
Your love flowing through me into them.

God's Fingerprints

God's fingerprints are on my life—
on the blessings I receive in abundance,
opportunities found in unwelcome change,
and miracles beyond my comprehension;

on the people He puts in my life,
the light He shines into my darkness,
and good He makes of my bad choices;

on the energy of my body,
the creativity of my mind,
and the fruits of my spirit.

State of Heart

Lord, give me a state of heart
that finds joy in ordinary things,
that treasures the beauty of Your creation,
that recognizes Godliness in each of Your children,
that achieves fulfillment in doing Your will,
that feels contentment with gifts already received,
that knows peace in Your love.

A State of Soul

Lord, give me a state of soul
that exudes generosity,
that embraces truth,
that manifests love,
that radiates hope,
that knows serenity,
that seeks eternity.

"Renew a Right Spirit Within Me"

A right spirit...
grieves the world's brokenness,
forgives unconditionally,
gives without an agenda,
chooses to be grateful,
reflects God's love,
knows pure joy.

My Soul's Perspective

When I see from my soul's perspective,
I welcome the opportunities in each new day,
I follow the path that God has prepared for me,
I embrace hope to triumph over fears,
I bless others with the gifts given me,
I rejoice in the goodness of creation and creator,
I know serenity in His merciful love.

Letting Go

When I let go of my will,
He guides me.
If I let go of my busy-ness,
He sustains me.
While I let go of my fears,
He comforts me.
Once I let go of my shame,
He forgives me.
When I let go, it's then
I let him love me.

My Prayer

I prayed.

I told God
what I wanted,
when I wanted it,
how I wanted it.

God answered
in His wisdom,
at His perfect time,
with what I needed.

Unanswered?

No prayer goes unanswered.
For in the waiting times,
God is preparing me
for an answer wiser
than any I could dream.

Healing Grace

I've prayed for healing,
but it does not come,
as it was with Paul
and Timothy too—
it is not God's will.

God has a purpose
I cannot discern
and a time table
unknown to mortals,
so I must accept
and rely on faith—
wisdom beyond mine,
His grace sufficient.

Wanting

I want to take control; God reminds me of my powerlessness.
I want to know the future; God offers me the serenity of surrender.
I want to find meaning; God puts people in my life to show me.
I want justice done; God blesses me with amazing grace.
I want to hide in my unworthiness; He showers me with unfathomable love.
For all I want, God gives me in abundance what I need.

Today

Today is the day the Lord has made,
filled with possibilities and opportunities
to see God in everyone and everything.
I will choose to glorify His name
and channel His love in word and deed.
For I am blessed to be a blessing.

Come into this World

Come, Holy Spirit,
breathe into this world
faith to sustain us,
peace to comfort us,
love to empower us.

Breath of the Spirit

Come, Holy Spirit,
breathe into my soul,
fill me with God's grace,
nurture a strong faith,
and empower me
to fulfill God's will.

46
47
53 God's Fingerprints
4

Made in the USA
Middletown, DE
18 December 2022

19278506R00040